Sepecat JAGUAR

By Glenn Ashley
Color by Don Greer
Illustrated by David Gebhardt
and Darren Glenn

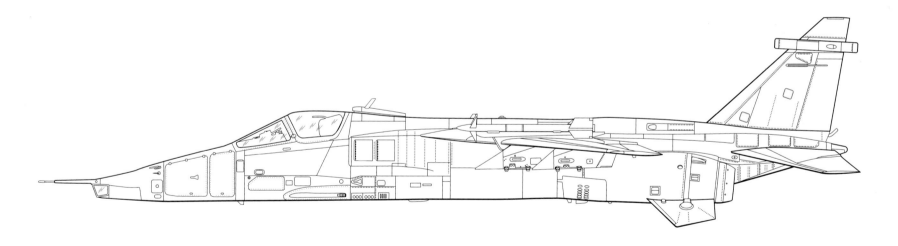

Aircraft Number 197

squadron/signal publications

"White Rose"(XZ3667/GP) an RAF GR.1 of No 54 Squadron hits fortified targets in Iraq

Acknowledgements

I would like to thank everyone who has contributed to this book in whatever means. The biggest thanks must go to the archive and public relations staff at BAe Warton for their kind help and constant support. Another big thanks goes to Paul Jackson for the use of his photographs.

And finally, I would to like to thank everyone else who has assisted in this title.

Picture Credits

British Aerospace

Tim Laming

Ministry of Defense

Tim Lewis

Sue Bushell

Military Aircraft Photographs

RAF Mildenhall Media Dept

Gary Madgwick

Neil Robinson

Wally Rouse

Rolls Royce Ltd.

Michael Hill

Jack Love

Paul Jackson

Brian Pickering

ECPA

Andy Evans

David James

ISBN 0-89747-491-0

If you have any photographs of aircraft, armor, soldiers or ships of any nation, particularly wartime snapshots, why not share them with us and help make Squadron/Signal's books all the more interesting and complete in the future. Any photograph sent to us will be copied and the original returned. The donor will be fully credited for any photos used. Please send them to:

Squadron/Signal Publications, Inc.
1115 Crowley Drive
Carrollton, TX 75011-5010

Если у вас есть фотографии самолётов, вооружения, солдат или кораблей любой страны, особенно, снимки времён войны, поделитесь с нами и помогите сделать новые книги издательства Эскадрон/Сигнал ещё интереснее. Мы переснимем ваши фотографии и вернём оригиналы. Имена приславших снимки будут сопровождать все опубликованные фотографии. Пожалуйста, присылайте фотографии по адресу:

Squadron/Signal Publications, Inc.
1115 Crowley Drive
Carrollton, TX 75011-5010

軍用機、装甲車両、兵士、軍艦などの写真を所持しておられる方はいらっしゃいませんか？どの国のものでも結構です。作戦中に撮影されたものが特に良いのです。Squadron/Signal社の出版する刊行物において、このような写真は内容を一層充実し、興味深くすることができます。当方にお送り頂いた写真は、複写の後お返しいたします。出版物中に写真を使用した場合は、必ず提供者のお名前を明記させて頂きます。お写真は下記にご送付ください。

Squadron/Signal Publications, Inc.
1115 Crowley Drive
Carrollton, TX 75011-5010

Banking in unison are four Jaguar GR.3s of No. 41 Squadron, Royal Air Force. Finished in the tactical Grey scheme now worn by the RAF Jaguar fleet, these workhorses have served the British well for over four decades. (Via David James)

3

Introduction

In the 30 years since its introduction into front-line military service the SEPECAT Jaguar has given sterling front-line service to several air arms around the World. Whenever it has been called into combat service it has shown excellent reliability as well as operational capabilities. Not a bad testament to an aircraft originally intended purely as an advanced trainer for use by the British and French air forces.

Its roots go back to a period when Great Britain and France worked very closely to produce several important Anglo-French types such as the Lynx, Gazelle and the best known – Concorde.

At the start of the 1960's both the Royal Air Force and Armee de l'Air were looking for a new advanced trainer that would enter service by the end of the decade. This new design had to be stable enough for a fairly inexperienced pilot to adapt to with a minimum of problems, but be advanced enough to be a challenging step up from basic trainers such as the Folland Gnat and Fouga Magister onto front-line types.

The British needs had been grouped together under the Air Staff Target 362 (AST362) which was put out to tender amongst the British aircraft manufacturers. Several companies responded including the Preston Division of the British Aircraft Corporation which featured variable geometry wings, indeed resembling what would look much akin to a later design, the Tornado. With stinging defense cuts by the British Labor Government, the development time and costs more than justified a swing wing aircraft, although following the cancellation of the TSR.2 the British were very close to purchasing the F-111K for RAF service. The other option was to cut development costs by joining forces with the French aviation industry.

The first prototype Jaguar was actually a two seater known to the French as a Jaguar 'E' and to the British as a 'B'. Here E.01 taxies out for an early test flight. The white 308 is actually the aircraft's allocated number for the 1969 Paris Air show at Le Bourget. Also worth noting is the large distinctive ejection warning triangles just below the cockpit. (BAe)

Although the main requirement for the French was for an advanced trainer, the ability to use the new aircraft as a lightweight combat aircraft would be an added bonus and this was taken into account when the French requirement was circulated around its own aviation companies. This requirement known as ECAT (Ecole de Combat d'Appui Tactique or Tactical Combat Trainer) had the same response as in the UK with the various companies responding in differing degrees. One company stood head and shoulders above the rest with no less than five different versions of the same design.

The Breguet BR.121 series seemed to have covered every possible role for the aircraft with the BR.121A – fighter-bomber, BR, 121B – a two seat version of the A, BR.121C – dedicated interceptor, BR.121E – advanced trainer and the BR.121P – reconnaissance version. It was this design that would become the backbone of the Jaguar design albeit, with a few changes along the way.

The joint agreements were signed in 1965 although the talks had started over a year before, and as well as jointly developing the new aircraft, officially called the Jaguar now, both nations would start work on a more advanced aircraft based upon the British Swing-Wing design, known as the AFVG (Anglo-French Variable Geometry) aircraft. Both nations were determined that the two aircraft be seen as carefully split projects with much of the work balanced out between the two countries, even down to the choice of engines.

Both nations agreed to order 150 aircraft each with the RAF, and Royal Navy, ordering only the two seat variations, France would have a 50/50 split of 75 trainers and 75 single seat combat support aircraft. But just over the horizon the plans would come off the rails for the British. As well as the cancelled orders for combat aircraft; the French did a 'U-turn' over the AFVG agreement by declaring the costs were too high. An odd and dubious statement considering that the funds originally intended for the AFVG were diverted into another independent project. In response to this sudden change in plans the British looked at how they could develop the concept and design into a frontline aircraft as well as trainer.

Prototype E.01 takes to the air as the landing gear retracts. The sleek lines of the Jaguar, even in its trainer form are obvious. The aircraft carries a split national insignia, half French, half British, often a style used when nations work together to develop an aircraft. (BAe)

On 9 January 1968 the British announced that they were now to order 200 Jaguars for the RAF with the naval interest declining rapidly. 90 of the new order were to be single seat strike versions, known as the Jaguar S, but this figure was increased in October 1970 to a much higher figure of 165. This left only 35 trainers for use with the RAF, a far cry from the original requirement.

Of the eight prototypes to be built the first five were all French built aircraft, the last three being built in Britain. The first prototype (E.01) was a two seater which made its first flight on 8 September 1968 from the airfield at Istres, piloted by Breguet's Chief Test Pilot Bernard Witt. The flight lasted some 25 minutes without any major faults in the handling. Indeed had the aircraft been ready a few weeks before it could well have made its debut at the SBAC shop at Farnborough that year.

The second prototype (E02), which was also a two seater, took to the air for the first time on 11 February 1969 from the same airfield with the same pilot at the controls. After a flight of around 65 minutes Witt declared himself very satisfied with the Jaguar in terms of ease to fly and the overall qualities of the aircraft. A03 was the first single seat Jaguar to be built, flying first on 29 March 1969. This aircraft had an initial flight that also lasted just over an hour, similar to that of E02, and again Witt reported that the single seat version handled very well indeed with, no changes to the aircraft compared to the two seater. The fourth prototype, A04, was a single seater too and would be used mainly for weapon trials. This flew for the first time on 27 May 1969. As can be seen all the French aircraft designated A are single seaters, those with E are two seaters.

M.05 was also a single seater, but differed greatly from all of the other Jaguars produced so far. It was built to specifications laid down by the French Navy who were considering using the aircraft aboard its carrier fleet. The main differences were in the undercarriage layout. The

nose wheel was a twin wheel arrangement with extendable leg and the main wheels were now single items. Other slight changes were made to the contours of the nose.

S06 was rolled out of the factory at Warton in Lancashire as the first British built Jaguar on 18 August 1969. This aircraft made its maiden flight on 12 October of that year from the companies own airfield. Piloted by Test pilot Jimmy Dell S06 went supersonic on its first flight, proof that the pilot had every confidence in the aircraft's ability and quality. The second British built Jaguar, S07, flew for the first time on 12 June 1970. The British only built one two seat prototype, B08, and this was taken aloft for its first flight on 30 August 1971.

By the time B08 flew the trials program was well under way with the first two aircraft, E.01 and E.02, being used basically to prove that the aircraft was aerodynamically up to the requirements. A03 was used for testing the navigation and attack systems that would be incorporated into the French built aircraft, as these differed from the British requirements, while A04 would actually be used to test fire all of the weapons that the Jaguar would contain in its portfolio of ordnance.

M05 was used for the carrier trials on both real and imitation carrier decks in both France and Britain. The trials involved the use of the "land based deck" at the Royal aircraft establishment base at Bedford in 1971. Sea trails being carried out aboard the Clemenceau in July of that year.

Of the British aircraft S06 was used for similar proving trials to the first two French aircraft, and on 23 February 1971 it undertook the first flight of a Jaguar between the two construction plants. The aircraft leaving Warton and landing at Istres one and a half hour later. S07 was the focus of the RAF's technical staff when they arrived at Warton to gain inside knowledge of the aircraft's systems. In 10 days they almost stripped the aircraft down completely

An overall view of the production line at BAe Warton in Lancashire. Several primer finished Jaguars, for the Indian Air Force, are being constructed. The darker areas on the upper surfaces are rubber mats that protect the aircraft's surface as well as giving non slip access for the workers. (BAe)

Developmental drawings

Jaguar A (French)

Jaguar GR.1A

Jaguar E (French)

Jaguar M

Jaguar GR.1 RAF

Jaguar GR.3

Jaguar T.2

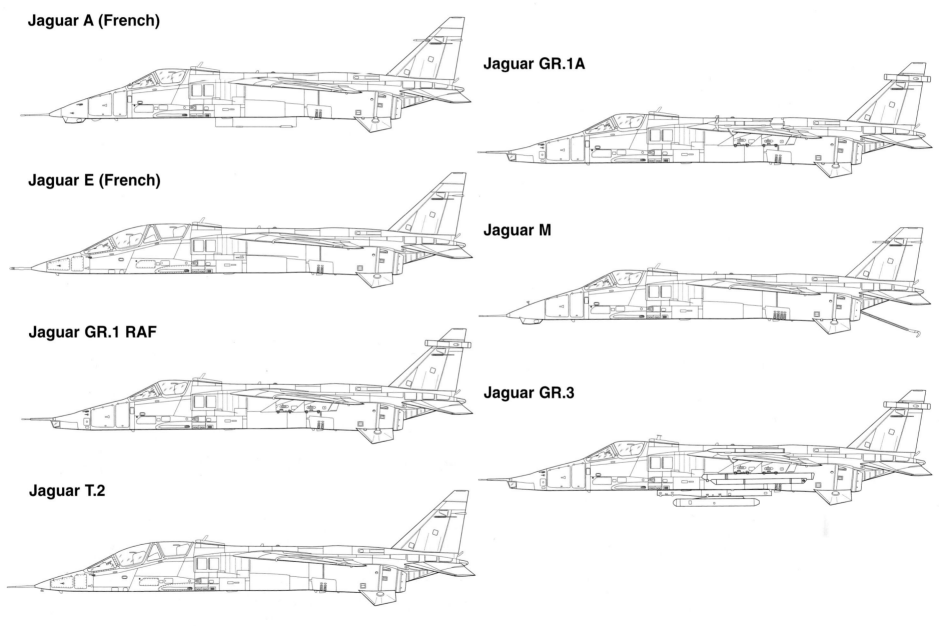

while a 20 man team carried out more than 200 different engineering tasks. The aim of these tasks was to make the support of the Jaguar as easy as possible for ground crews when it entered service.

B08 was built completely from production parts and so in all but name was a full production Jaguar. It wa used to prove the production standard of the company and aircraft. Amongst the trials carried out by B08 were the rough field trials while carrying a varied selection of weapons and other stores. This must have been quite a sight, an aircraft taxiing through grass that came above the tops of the wheels while carrying a full weapon load. The Jaguar was seen as ideal for operations from unprepared strips in time of war as could be seen from the stalky but rugged construction of the undercarriage, something often overlooked by Western aircraft designers but usually a key feature of Warsaw Pact designed aircraft.

As the trials came to a successful conclusion the first production aircraft were already on the assembly lines in both France and Great Britain. The first production aircraft for the Armee de l'Air was flown for the first time on 2 November 1971 from the Toulouse/Blagnac Airport while the first British production aircraft did not fly until 12 October 1972 from Warton.

Almost immediately as the aircraft began to enter service with the RAF the aircraft underwent modifications that made them differ in appearance to the French aircraft. The nose was fitted with a new chisel shaped replacement that housed the Ferranti laser system aimed at giving the Jaguar the most accurate weapon delivery system in Europe. Once weapons had been selected the onboard computer would continually correct and adjust to give the pilot the best chance of taking out a target the first time round.

So by the time the Jaguar entered service with both nations it was a very potent piece of equipment that would give several decades of valuable and reliable service.

Jaguar A/GR.1

When originally conceived, it was intended that the first production Jaguars would enter service by the end of 1970 with the Armee de l'Air, and by 1975 with the RAF. As is the norm with any complicated piece of equipment there were the usual delays and teething troubles that affect the development of any new aircraft. These in turn delay the date of entry into squadron service, with the Jaguar this was to happen more than other types as both nations involved had changing needs and numbers required.

Parked in front of a French Hardened Aircraft Shelter (HAS), is A156/7-NB of EC 4/7. This unit was actually the last to equip with the Jaguar A. The French aircraft carries a laser nose and lacks the fin mounted RWR carried by RAF aircraft. (Paul Jackson)

French Service

The deliveries to the Armee de l'Air began on 24 May 1973 when the first batch of aircraft arrived at St Dizier as replacements for aging Mystere IV's operated by No: 1 Escadron of the 7th Escadre de Chase. This arrival of new aircraft came shortly after the unit had moved to a new location, so it took a little while before the air and ground crews were familiar with both the new generation aircraft and the surroundings in which it operated.

The next two units to equip with the Jaguar A were both part of the 7th Escadre de Chase, being EC 3/7 and EC 2/7. EC 3/7 received the first aircraft on 14 March 1974 and EC 2/7 on 1 May 1974. The intention had been to gradually build up the Jaguar force at a rate of some 28-30 aircraft per year.

At the same time that the Jaguar was being prepared for frontline service seven aircraft, two Jaguar As and five Jaguar Es, were assigned to the Centre d'Experiences Aeriennes Militaires (CEAM) at Mont-de-Marsan. They were to formulate the operational guidelines for the aircraft once it entered service, very much on par with the role carried out by the British at Boscombe Down. Once the CEAM were happy the Jaguar units would, once up to full strength, declare themselves operationally ready.

The founding 7th Escadre de Chase and its three sub components found themselves straight in at the sharp end of the French deterrent with EC 1/7 and 3/7 assigned to the role of delivery of tactical nuclear weapons using the AN52 special weapon. EC 2/7 would, in peacetime, be used as a training unit but in times of conflict it became a fully combat ready unit serving in the conventional support role at both low and medium altitudes.

Early in 1975 the next Escadre de Chase began to form with EC 3/11 who received its first aircraft on 7 February. The role of EC 3/11 was vastly removed from that of the earlier units as it was intended that the unit would carry out what used to be called gunboat diplomacy. The unit could, and would, deploy to any region of the world where French interests were under threat. It would be hoped that this rapid deployment of the latest combat aircraft would calm down any underlying intentions for revolt.

Later that year EC 1/11 was formed in October. Their role was purely one of supplying tactical support for French land forces in Europe. Although France was no longer a NATO member it still retained strong links with NATO when it came to a united front in the stand against the threat of attack from Warsaw Pact forces. Had war broken out across Europe EC

Taxiing along the perimeter track is Jaguar A, A27/3-XP of EC 3/3 during the early 1980's. This unit flew the type between 1977 and 1987 while based at Nancy/Ochey. During this time the unit flew Jaguars on missions against the Libyan airfield in Chad. (Author Collection).

The cockpit of a single seat Jaguar A/GR.1. Fairly typical of the designs of the period, uncluttered with easy access to all controls for the pilot. The interior is finished in black. Note the lack of TV monitors and other state of the art systems, the cockpit would be improved as part of the Jaguar'96 upgrade. (BAe).

1/11 would give close air support to the French 1st Army using both the 30mm cannon and a varied selection of bombs.

When EC 2/11 formed at Toule/Rosieres on 3 November 1976 they were given yet another role for the Jaguar, this time one of ECM and enemy defense suppression. These "Wild Weasel" Jaguars did not actually begin to carry out this role until some time later. The aircraft carry the Martel anti-radiation missile for this type of sortie and the EC 2/11 aircraft were the first to be fitted with a laser range finder mounted on the underside of the nose. On close range sorties the aircraft would carry the Martel on the centerline pylon and ECM gear in pods under the wings. For missions over a much longer distance the aircraft would be fitted with under wing tanks or be given tanker support for in flight refueling.

EC 4/11 completed the Escadre 11 formation. This unit formed at Bordeaux on 1 August 1978 replacing the ageing F-100 Super Sabre. EC 4/11 along with EC 4/7, who formed on 1 April 1980, were attached to 2 CATc, a rapid reaction force that could deploy anywhere in the World to give military support to French interests. And this they would do on a number of occasions.

The French aircraft differ from their British counterparts in a number of ways. The French Jaguar A has a lower grade of avionics than the RAF GR.1 but it was still a potent aircraft. For a number of years the French did not feel that the aircraft would benefit from a laser range finder, but in later production aircraft the Thomson-CSF TAV-38 laser is fitted, along with a camera, in a pod under the nose. The laser system was further enhanced by the introduction of the Automatic Tracking Laser Illumination System (ATLIS) which is carried on the centerline pylon. This has increased the quality of the weapon load that can be fitted to the aircraft. Some 30 aircraft have been equipped to carry ATLIS but the system can be linked to the MATRA 1000lb Laser Guided Bomb and the Aerospatiale AS30L Air to Surface Missile. Only one ASM is carried, normally under the starboard wing with the aircraft balanced by a drop tank under the port wing.

Other weaponry often carried by Armee de l'Air Jaguars includes the MATRA AS37 Martel anti radar missile, MATRA LR.F2 rocket pods, BAP 100-mm runway denial bombs, MATRA F1 rockets and AN52 nuclear weapon.

Sharing the stage for the Jaguars 20th Anniversary are two Armee de l'Air As. On the left is A29/11-MB of EC2/11, and on the right is A48/7-EC of EC1/11. Apart from the special schemes both styles of French camouflage can be seen here. The tricolor is carried on the fin and rear fuselage and ventral fin, along with a Jaguar's head artwork. (Paul Jackson)

Sepecat

Jaguar A French

General Arrangement

Powerplant	Two Rollls Royce Tubomeca Mk 104s
Maximum Speed	990 m.p.h.
Weight Empty	15,430 lb
Max.Weight Take Off	34,175 lb
Span	28 ft 6 in
Length	55 ft 3 in
Height	16 ft 2 in
Armament	Two 30mm DEFA 553 Cannons Up to 4 AIM 9 Sidewinder Missiles

During operations in Chad and the 1991 Gulf War variations of different weaponry were seen to be carried by French Jaguars for both offensive and defensive reasons.

As well as the frontline units and the CEAM another French operator exists, the Centre d'Essais en Vol (CEV). The CEV carries out many tests on both an aircraft's airworthiness, and to a lesser degree weapon trials. The airworthiness tests are carried out from its base at Bretigny-sur-Orge with weapon testing at Cazaux. The unit operates both single seat prototypes, A03 and A04, as well as the two seat prototype E.01.

British Service

The Royal Air Force took delivery of its first Jaguars on 13 September 1973 at RAF Lossiemouth where a conversion course was jointly run by the RAF and British Aircraft Corporation in order to get both air and ground crews trained on the aircraft. The aircraft would not become operational until the following year when No. 54 Sqn formed at Lossiemouth on 5 June 1974. The Jaguar was on schedule for its introduction into the frontline make up of the RAF at the time.

The same day saw an aircraft also painted in the markings of No. 6 Sqn and this aircraft was fitted with the new laser rangefinder, an obvious signal as to which unit would be the second to form. Indeed 6 November that year saw the formation of the unit when the F-4 Phantoms were traded in for the smaller lighter aircraft. Lossiemouth would remain the base for conversion unit for the Jaguar but other frontline units would move south to Norfolk and RAF Coltishall. The RAF planned to base three units at Coltishall and also operate a further five as part of RAF Germany, where the British were a major factor in NATO's frontline defense against the Warsaw Pact.

No. 6 Sqn took up residence at Coltishall late in 1974 with a role of supplying close support for mobile British units that may be required to deploy to hotspots around the World. These aircraft were fitted with the Ferranti ARI 23231 laser guidance unit. This was mounted in a re-designed wedge shaped glazed nose that replaced the earlier pointed nose cone. This immediately made the British Jaguars distinguishable from the French ones by the new nose shape. Another modification was the addition of a fin mounted RWR pod giving the aircraft a little more self defense.

The early part of 1975 saw the first units form in Germany. No. 14 Sqn formed at RAF Bruggen on 7 April with No. 17 Sqn two months later. The RAFG aircraft would have an expanded role over the UK based units by adding to their close support role with that of battlefield reconnaissance. Also should the situation arise the aircraft would be capable of carrying and using tactical nuclear weapons against enemy forces. The third unit to form was No. 31 Sqn, also at Bruggen and following the formation of No. 2 Sqn the three earlier units became dedicated attack squadrons, with No. 2, based at RAF Laarbruch, which would be a purely reconnaissance unit.

In order to carry out battlefield reconnaissance the Jaguar would carry a centerline recce pod that resembled a fuel tank, but was in fact crammed with various photographic and infrared information gathering equipment. It was a role originally conceived for the cancelled TSR.2 many years before.

Back in the UK another recce unit formed, No. 41 Sqn, based at Coltishall. But in the event of war in Europe the unit would deploy to Norway as part of NATO's northern flank. The final part of the jigsaw was completed when No. 20 Sqn formed at Bruggen on 28 February 1977 trading in its Harrier GR.3s for the Jaguar. This completed the build up of the

Lined up on the runway, ready for take off, are three Armee de l'Air Jaguar As. All three carry 11 bombs on the various under wing and centerline pylons. This would be a typical weapon load for a short range mission if war had broken out in Europe. Also clearly seen is the landing light mounted in the nose wheel door. (BAe)

Refueled and ready for take off A29/11-MB sits on the ramp during the Jaguar's 20th Anniversary festivities in 1993. The nose is black while the cat head begins the two shades of brown that continues on to the tail. The tricolor is also carried on the upper wing tips.

The RAF GR.1 has always been a steady performer for the British. This GR.1 from No. 54 Sqn is parked on the pan at RAF Waddington in 1990. It carries the standard under wing tanks, ECM pod and bombs under the centerline pylon. The chisel nose and RWR fairings fitted to the British aircraft are very evident here. (Author)

Banking over a lake in Germany is XX959/CJ of No. 20 Sqn based at Bruggen. The aircraft is fitted with the standard centerline tank and pair of 1,000lb practice LGB's. At least one new airbrake has been fitted as can be seen by the camouflage not matching. The weathered undersides of the aircraft are evident. The Jaguar played an important role in NATO's defense in Germany. (BAe)

XX955/AN from No. 14 Sqn drops four practice bombs during a training sortie. Still carrying four on the under wing pylons this shows the maximum bomb load that the Jaguar could carry, on short distance sorties since no under wing tanks can be carried. The practice bombs have the forward sections painted Medium Blue. (BAe)

GR.1A of No. 41 Sqn parked in the display area at the RAF's 75th Anniversary in 1993. This immaculate aircraft, XZ356/R, was also known as 'Mary Rose' during the 1991 Gulf War flying 33 missions against Iraqi positions. It still retains its over wing AIM-9 Sidewinders, not usually carried on UK based Jaguars. (Author)

Arming the Jaguar is not difficult for ground crews due to the high undercarriage making the underside of the aircraft readily accessible. This RAF armorer puts a 500lb bomb under the centerline pylon of a GR.1A. The bomb trolley raises the weapon into position. (Paul Jackson)

A trio of No. 6 Sqn aircraft in formation over the North Sea. All carry different weapon loads. Nearest to the camera, XX962/EK carries an LGB on the centerline, under wing tanks and AIM-9 Sidewinders. XX725/EL has a centerline tank, LGB and ECM Pod and XX270/EN carries the tank, a 1,000lb Iron Bomb and ECM Pod. (BAe)

GR.1, XZ400/EG, of No. 6 Sqn on a post Gulf war sortie. Finished in the standard low Vis camouflage the aircraft is fitted with Desert camouflaged tanks. Just forward of the canopy is the black painted anti-glare panel and for its age the jaguar still retains a sleek profile in the sky. (Paul Jackson)

Departing RAF Marham in 1993 is GR.1A, XX766/EC, of No. 6 Sqn with both afterburners lit. The aircraft also carries the over wing AIM-9 Sidewinder rails and missiles. (Author)

aircraft as part of RAF Germany.

The role of the Jaguar was a key part of a three stage response to any Warsaw Pact aggression. The Harriers would be in forward operating bases directly behind the frontlines, the Jaguars would deploy to forward bases or suitable stretches of autobahns, and the third line was one of Buccaneers and Vulcan's who would operate from conventional airbases some distance behind the frontlines. By deploying aircraft like the Jaguar and Harrier to these kinds of locations in smaller groups would possibly have given them a little more survivability as major airfields would be high up on a list of enemy targets.

During its career as part of the RAF's frontline service the Jaguar was updated in order to keep the aircraft as current as possible to meet any ongoing requirements. The 1980's saw advancements in the Internal Navigation System (INS) computer to the extent that an entire mission could be planned in the squadron HQ, fed into the memory pod of the INS and when this was fitted to the aircraft all course details, and any other relevant data, were displayed on the pilots Head Up Display (HUD). This left the pilot more time to concentrate on the job in hand, such as looking for targets or surface to air threats.

One area where the RAF aircraft have lagged behind the French ones is that they have never been updated to allow the fitting of Air to Surface missiles like their French counterparts. These new additions saw the aircraft now designated as GR.1As in RAF service. As far as self defense goes the GR.1A can carry the Westinghouse AN/ALQ-101 Jamming Pod, Philips-

Taxiing along the perimeter track at RAF Alconbury is XX965/07 of No. 226 OCU. This unit is used for pilot's conversion courses onto the Jaguar from other aircraft such as the Hawk, seen taking off behind. This aircraft was used as the RAF's display Jaguar and has its fin painted black breaking up the normal camouflage. The aircraft does not carry any under wing stores during its display and the stalky undercarriage of the Jaguar is very evident. (Author)

In times of war in Western Europe the Jaguar would operate alongside Harrier forces, as proven in combat over Yugoslavia. In the sweltering heat at RAF Mildenhall Harriers and Jaguars sit parked ready to show the crowd how they work together in action. A Jaguar GR.1A from No. 226 OCU waits along with a trio of Harrier GR.5's from No. 233 OCU. (Author)

Celebrating the 75th Anniversary of No. 41 Sqn the Commanding Officer's mount has been given a new dash of color. The spine is finished in red with a white trim. Who says you can't pull rank! (Paul Jackson)

Stripped down and ready to be upgraded and repainted. A very sorry looking Jaguar sits in a hangar at RAF Abingdon awaiting the completion of the upgrade program and a fresh coat of paint. The nose mounted laser finder has been removed on this aircraft as well as a number of panels from the upper fuselage. (Paul Jackson)

Not all Jaguars ended up with being part of the upgrade program. This one ended up as a ground instructional machine at RAF Cosford. Here it is kept hangared for RAF trainee's to learn their trade. Note the Wise Owl with mortar board badge applied to the tail of this aircraft. (Author)

With the changing times a change in camouflage. The traditional Grey/Green was replaced with a new overall grey scheme that also saw changes in the national insignia during the 1990's. These four aircraft from No. 41 Sqn carry the new scheme. The reduction in size of the national insignia and also now only a single roundel is carried on the upper port wing. The new schemes were usually applied when the aircraft went in for the Jaguar upgrade program. (Via David James)

Out with the old, in with the new! A pair of No. 54 Sqn Jaguar GR.1As on a training mission in 1995. At this time the RAF fleet was being upgraded and repainted.

XX723/GQ wears the standard scheme that the aircraft carried from the 1970's while XX722/GB is finished in the new scheme. (D. Cubitt via David James)

MATRA Phimat chaff dispensers and Tracor AN/ALE-40 flare dispensers. Very rarely fitted are the over wing rails which allow the carrying of one AIM-9 Sidewinder above each wing. If these were not fitted sometimes a single AIM-9 could be carried on an outer pylon, with an ALQ-101 on the same pylon on the other wing.

With all this extra weight being hauled across the skies the engines would have to be up rated or replaced in order to keep the aircraft at the top end of its combat capabilities so from 1978 onwards the original Ardour mk.102 engines were replaced by the newer mk.804 versions which were normally fitted to the export aircraft. This engine was called the RT172-26 engine within the RAF and made a significant improvement to the power of the Jaguar.

During the start of the 1990's the world saw the collapse of the Warsaw Pact as communism fell by the wayside across Europe and so the Jaguar seemed destined for a quiet end to its front line service with no recognizable enemy on the continent. The RAF began to replace the Jaguar with newer designs such as the Tornado, a task that had started in the mid 1980's as the new aircraft entered service with Jaguars going into storage or for use as ground training aircraft. But history would soon change that and the Jaguar found it still had a vital role to play in world events.

Resplendent in their new grey scheme which highlights the unit colors; these four aircraft are from No. 41 Sqn. The aircraft nearest is presumably the CO's mount as it has white edged fin and notes of the 85th Anniversary of the unit, formed in 1916. The nearest aircraft does not have a black painted fin top. (Via David James)

(Below) High above the clouds is GR.1A, XZ364/GJ, of No. 54 Sqn finished in the overall grey scheme introduced in the mid 1990's. The Blue/Yellow checks and prancing lion squadron badge is clearly seen. (Via David James)

(Above) A toned down GR.3, XX745/D, from No. 16 Sqn flies low over a forest area, possibly in Scotland during a training sortie. The aircraft carried practice bomb carriers under the outer pylons which are green in color and it still carries Green/Grey camouflaged under wing tanks. No. 16 Sqn is a split unit which operates in conjunction with No. 226 OCU. (Via David James)

Up into the blue yonder goes GR.3, XX117/A, of No. 16 Sqn/226 OCU. Note the tartan trim running along the RWR on the fin. Since toning down the scheme the serials and national insignia have also been reduced in size. (Via David James)

Jaguars from four different units gather in formation. At the top is an aircraft from No. 16 Sqn/226 OCU with the familiar 'Saint' badge on the fin. Next is an aircraft from No. 54 Sqn fitted with overwing Sidewinder rails, then we have an example from No. 41 Sqn and finally No. 6 Sqn. Note the variation in weapon fits including the Recce Pod under the 41 Sqn aircraft. (Via David James)

Motorway Trials

With the undercarriage of the Jaguar being very rugged in order that it can operate from less than ideal surfaces such as unprepared runways it became obvious from the start that in time of war the aircraft would be capable of operating from improvised airstrips utilizing suitable stretches of a motorway. The idea had been proven by air forces in Switzerland and Scandinavia, so why not Britain, France or the front line in West Germany?

The thought was that in the event of a conflict between the Warsaw Pact and NATO some of the first targets to be damaged or destroyed would be major airfields. This was something already considered in the design of most Soviet combat aircraft, but not in the West and would give WARPAC forces a distinct advantage. As the Jaguar was the only conventional aircraft capable of being used from unprepared strips or motorways the British Aircraft Corporation decided to undertake a series of trials on the unopened stretch of the M55 motorway near Blackpool, not very far from the Warton factory.

On 26-27 April 1975 a single Jaguar GR.1, XX109, was used to make a series of landings and take offs from the M55 carrying a full weapon load, after all an unarmed aircraft would prove nothing. Landing took just over 400 yards to complete with the assistance of a braking parachute whilst take off was carried out in 500-600 yards.

The first landings were undertaken with only a centerline tank fitted and the aircraft was turned around, fuelled and armed with four cluster bomb units before taking off again. The pilot for these trials was Tim Ferguson, the Deputy Chief Test Pilot, who stated that the trials threw up no major problems.

The aircraft had to make a steep approach and high angle landing using the bulk of the aircraft as well as the braking chute to bring the aircraft to a halt in the short length of motorway. He stated that as the Jaguar had excellent steering and handling the landing was not overly complicated.

Following the success of the trials four RAF Germany aircraft from No. 31 Sqn undertook similar trials on an unopened stretch of autobahn between Bremerhaven and Bremen in September 1977.

Another series of trials were undertaken by the A&AEE at Boscombe Down using a landing strip that crossed a runway, two taxiways with various elements added to make the surface very uneven. It seems the pilots soon became capable of taking off and landing on this strip with a feeling described as being like a "well sprung limousine with four wheel drive".

Jaguar GR.1, XX109, lifts off the M55 motorway near Blackpool in April 1975 during trials to see how suitable the Jaguar was for this kind of use in wartime. The aircraft carries four inert bombs and a standard centerline tank. There would be no point doing these tests without the aircraft carrying a full weapon load in order to gauge take off lengths. (BAe)

Completing a successful landing back on the M55 having dispersed its war load to show the true landing speed and distance of post-sortie landings. Even the agile Jaguar required the aid of a braking chute to minimize its landing distance. (BAe)

Hammering down the motorway, and no danger of a speeding ticket! XX109 starts its take off run. The short distance made evident by the curve in the road further ahead. (BAe)

Jaguar Trainers

With the decision to develop the Jaguar into a single seat strike aircraft there was a great reduction in the number of two seat training versions required by both the French and British air forces.

Both nations had their own designation for the trainer, in France it was the Jaguar E and in Britain the Jaguar B initially, the RAF later redesignating it the T.2. There were more physical changes, due partly to internal political requirements to suit home suppliers. The Jaguar E was to be armed with two DEFA 30mm cannon, very basic navigation systems and Martin-Baker mk.IV ejection seats. The Jaguar T.2 on the other hand was to be fitted with the same navigation/attack system as the GR.1, Martin-Baker mk.IX seats but only one Aden cannon.

French Service

With a slightly reduced requirement of only 40 trainers the French made these priority production over the single seat variant giving the chance to put pilots through a conversion course in time for the delivery of the first Jaguar As. The first production trainer, E1, flew for the first time on 2 November 1971 with deliveries starting early in 1972 with nine aircraft being delivered by the end of the year. The following year saw the number grow, and as each unit exchanged its outgoing aircraft with the new ones they received a mix of single and twin seat Jaguars. The French did not operate a dedicated conversion unit for the type, unlike the RAF.

The first aircraft were delivered to the Centre d'Experiences Aeriennes Militaires (CEAM) whose task it was to define the role of the Jaguar in Armee de l'Air service, giving guidelines to each unit that would operate the aircraft. As pilots came to exchange their mounts, the ageing Mystere IV, they undertook a short course on the Jaguar E before the units became fully operational. The first to undertake this was EC 1/7 followed by the remaining squadrons in EC 7. This procedure would continue until all the front line units were fully equipped with the type both single and twin seaters. The Es would remain on strength for future pilots to undertake conversion courses within the units themselves which should speed up conversion as the pilots would be familiarizing themselves with both the aircraft and the unit at the same time.

As their courses got underway a number of questions were raised about the variations between the A and E models which meant that transition from the E onto the A was not quite as simple as had been originally thought. It seemed the cost cutting carried out in the planning of the program was a little short sighted.

The Jaguar E has had a steady if un-exciting service life with the Armee de l'Air continuing to give reliable service to its parent units without a great deal of publicity or fanfare, often the case with an aircraft that has a good safety record performing what could be described as mundane day to day duties.

A number of Jaguar Es have been lost to accidents as happens with any aircraft and as part of military defense cuts a number have been placed in storage. This meant that by 1992 there were only 25 Es remaining operational from the original 40 ordered. It is likely that as the Rafale enters full service the remaining aircraft will also slip by the wayside, into storage, or maybe passed onto a friendly nation?

British Service

Unlike the Armee de l'Air the RAF intended that the Jaguar T.2 should be capable of carrying out operational missions in time of conflict working alongside the GR.1 so in all aspects apart from the second seat the T.2 was identical to the GR.1 in terms of capabilities. One major difference that both the E and T.2 had in common that differed from the single seat versions was that neither was fitted with the internal in-flight refueling (IFR) probe thus restricting their range to fuel that could be carried internally or in under wing tanks. This was not seen as a problem because if you are in such a situation that you are having to utilize trainers as front-line combat aircraft you already have your backs to the wall without having to go far to find the enemy.

The first T.2's to enter service with the RAF included a sole example that was delivered to the Jaguar Conversion team (JCT) which formed in 1973 in preparation for the aircraft's entry into service. The T.2, XX137, was delivered to the JCT in September 1974. Further aircraft followed including a number of GR.1's with the unit being used to train up the first crews of No. 54 Sqn who would be the RAF's first Jaguar operator.

The Jaguars of the JCT were absorbed into No. 54 Sqn when it formed and many of the JET assets were passed onto No. 226 Operational Conversion Unit (OCU) which formed at RAF Lossiemouth in October 1974 with the task of undertaking all conversion training for RAF Jaguar pilots as well as doing a similar task with the overseas nations who purchased the Jaguar. The OCU operated a mixture of GR.1 and T.2 aircraft and as the unit grew in size alongside the number of Jaguar squadrons it was itself split into two squadrons, No. 1 and No. 2, of the OCU with overall control kept together under the OCU umbrella.

In keeping with the aircraft's secondary role as a strike aircraft in time of war the aircraft

Running up to full power at night creates a very impressive image. The prototype Jaguar E02 turns up the heat in early trials. This aircraft was used extensively for engine trials as part of the development program. (BAe)

Taxiing in at an airbase in France is Jaguar E E6/11-ME of EC 2/11. Even the trainers in this unit are finished in the Sand/Brown desert scheme. In the harsh desert climate the Brown had a tendency to fade quite badly, but providing a much more subtle camouflage effect. (Paul Jackson)

EC 3/11 have flown Jaguars since 1975 and have seen service in hotspots across Africa and the Middle East. This standard camouflaged E 11-AF gets the attention of a ground crew member. EC 3/11's SPA69 badge, worn on the starboard side of the fin, has often been noted as being somewhat sexually explicit, as a closer inspection would reveal! (Paul Jackson)

The CEV carries out military trials for the French AF and among the types flown is the Jaguar. A two seater drops a pair of 1,000lb Lazer Guided Bombs during a test flight from Cazaux. (Paul Jackson)

Sepecat
Jaguar GR.1(RAF)

General Arrangement

Powerplant	Two Rollls Royce Tubomeca Mk 104s
Maximum Speed	1,056 m.p.h.
Weight Empty	15,432 lb
Max.Weight Take Off	34,000 lb
Span	28 ft 6 in
Length	50 ft 11 in
Height	16 ft 2 in
Armament	Two 30mm Aden Cannons Up to 4 AIM 9 Sidewinder Missiles

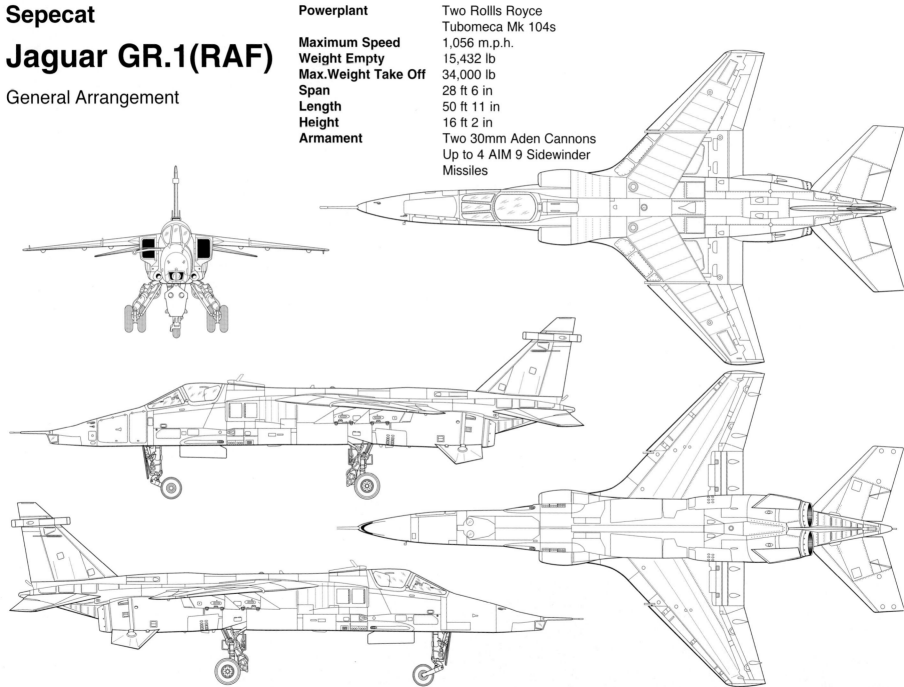

were finished in standard RAF camouflage and the instructors were kept up to date with weapon training. The OCU was not just a glorified flying school for trainee Jaguar drivers. In time of war the unit's aircraft would be deployed to join frontline units and bolster their numbers. For this reason they were not given shadow squadron status. This changed in 1991 when as part of the RAF withdrawal from Germany No. 16 Sqn disbanded and relinquished its Tornado GR.1's to become the shadow number for the OCU.

In a slightly different way to the Armee de l'Air units all RAF frontline Jaguar squadrons have at least one T.2 on strength for various reasons, including a degree of conversion training although the bulk is done by the OCU.

During the upgrading in the mid 1980s all GR.1 and T.2 aircraft were fitted with the newer Ferranti FIN 1064 navigation/attack system replacing the Marconi-Elliott NAVWASS system. As aircraft were modified they were redesignated GR.1A and T.2A making both versions amongst the most advanced strike aircraft in Europe. The future of the T.2 being secured as long as the single seaters were in service.

As well as the RAF a small number of T.2/2As have been operated by other bodies within the Ministry of Defense (MoD). The Empire Test Pilots School (ETPS) based at Boscombe Down has been responsible for training test pilots from all over the World and operates just about every type that is in service with the British Armed Forces. They operate two T.2As, XX145 and XX830, amongst their fleet. These replaced two earlier aircraft, XX915 and XX916, which were both lost in accidents during the early 1980's. These along with the aircraft from the A&AEE and DRA are the most colorful Jaguars trainers to date being finished in Red, White and Blue schemes.

The Airplane & Armament Experimental Establishment (A&AEE) is also based at Boscombe Down and has operated two T.2s. The A&AEE has been responsible over the years for testing the upgrades and modifications made to the Jaguar during its career. The home of the other colorful Jaguar is at Farnborough where the Defense Research Agency (DRA), formerly the Royal Aircraft Establishment, is based. They have two jaguars on strength, T.2, ZB615, and T.2A XX835.

Another T.2A is operated by the Strike/Attack Operational Evaluation Unit which is based at Boscombe Down and this unit also flies Harriers and Tornados. The unit is responsible for gaining operational experience with FLIR used in the Harrier GR.7 and Tornado GR.4.

Considering the capability of the Jaguar T.2/E series, it seems remarkable that nobody has ever considered using the aircraft as a Forward Air Controller (FAC) or in a Wild Weasel role, much like the F-16 has been developed. But, with the aircraft still very active in many aspects, who knows what could be round the corner?

Flaring in to land is Jaguar E 11-AD of the CEAM based at Mont-de-Marsan. Unlike the RAF aircraft the French Jaguars have retained their Silver underside color seen clearly here. As the CEAM completed the trials with the Jaguars they passed the aircraft on to front line units of the Armee de l'Air. The wide swept undercarriage shows the rugged construction of it. (Paul Jackson)

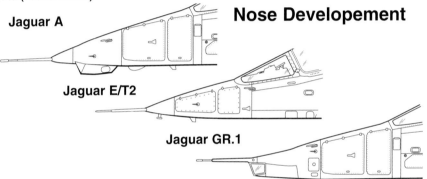

On its take off run from RAF Marham in 1993 is Jaguar T.2A 'J' from No. 226 OCU, but wearing the markings of its shadow unit No. 16 Sqn. The RAF two seaters adopted the full wrap round camouflage scheme of the single seaters. The landing light is mounted in the nose wheel door. (Author)

Getting airborne from Warton is a Jaguar T.2 in the early scheme worn by the type with the Light Grey undersides. The aircraft is carrying a mixed load of 1,000lb bombs along with a centerline tank. (BAe)

Jaguar Prototype with the standard grey/green/light blue camouflage.

Jaguar GR.1 XX726 of No.41 Squadron, known as the "Flying Canopeners" denoting their prowess against armor.

French Jaguar A of EC 1/11 "Roussillon" deployed to Chad in support of the government against Libyan supported insurgents. The scheme is dark brown and light sand over light blue.

EC I/11 "Roussillon"

Jaguar GR.1A of No.41 Squadron with temporary white camouflage over the green leaving a grey back ground. The 1A carried missiles mounted on the upper wing.

GR.1A, XZ364/GJ of No.54 Squadron in an overall grey finish which was introduced in the mid 1990s. XZ364/GJ also carries low vis markings.

Squadron Badge of No.54 Squadron

Jaguar GR.Mk1A (XZ364) of the detachment from RAF Coltishall Wing based at Muharraq, Bahrain. Sadman is one of two aircraft to fly 47 missions. "Sadman" carries a full coat of temporary desert pink.

"Sadman"

Jaguar A of EC 4/11, part of the French force participation in the Gulf War under OPERATION DAGUET. 11-4Y is painted in wrap around gray and sand.

Jaguar A GR.1 of the Federal Nigerian Air Force.

Jaguar A of EC II/7 "Provence" with the new French wrap around desert scheme of light brown and sand used in the Gulf War.

EC II/7 "Provence"

No.41 Sdn Flying "Can Openers"

Overall grey GR.3s of No.41 Squadron joined Harrier GR.5s carrying out missions in Yugoslavia during the Kosovo conflict.

(Right) The same aircraft powers into the sky with both afterburners lit. Note the lack of RWR on the fin and also this T.2 does not have the Laser Rangefinder built into the nose, reducing the combat capability of the trainer version. (Author)

(Below) T.2 XX829/ET, of No. 6 Sqn carrying modified tail markings. The title is 'Flying Canopeners', a reference to the attack capability of the squadron. (Paul Jackson)

Sepecat
Jaguar T.2

Powerplant	Two Rollls Royce Tubomeca Mk 104s
Maximum Speed	1,056 m.p.h.
Weight Empty	15,432 lb
Max.Weight Take Off	34,000 lb
Span	38 ft 6 in
Length	35 ft 11 in
Height	16 ft 2 in
Armament	One 30mm Aden Cannon

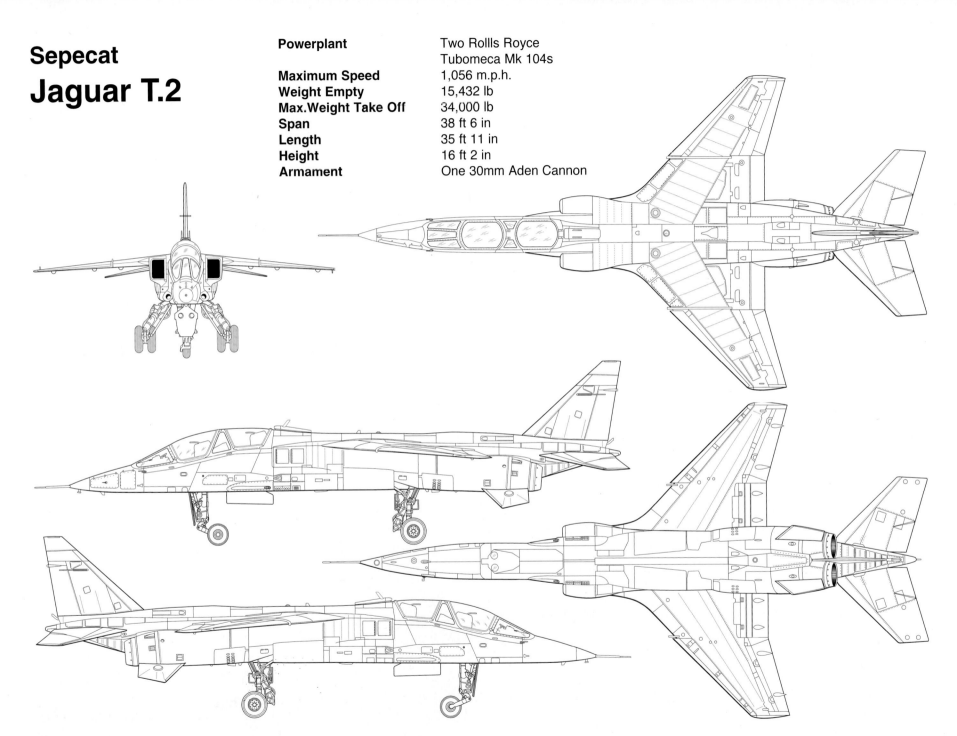

Naval Trials

At the time of the development stages of the Jaguar a sole aircraft that incorporated a number of modifications was built. Designated the Jaguar M the type was to conduct trials to look at the possibility of the aircraft being operated by the French Navy from its aircraft carriers. The Jaguar M would be capable of carrying out lightweight strike operations and appeared ideally suited to the role with its strong undercarriage, ability to carry a useful weapon load, and also the lower cost, and that development was well underway. Politically it was a better option than having to purchase aircraft from the US.

The Jaguar M differed from the S by way of having an extendable twin nose wheel, single main wheels on strengthened undercarriage legs. Also it was fitted with a 5.5-G capable arrestor hook and catapult fittings under the lower forward fuselage.

The sole Jaguar M, M05/F-ZWRJ, made its first flight on 14 November 1969 at Melun-Villaroche with an initial flight lasting about an hour. Once the basic flight testing was done the aircraft was flown to Bedford in England for trials on the land based deck set up there. The trials were a successful and so the aircraft proceeded to the next stage, full sea trials.

For the purpose of sea trials the French Navy had made the carrier Clemenceau available, and on 8 July the Jaguar M made its first true carrier deck landing. For the next couple of days checks were made to see that no stress damage had been inflicted on the aircraft and on 10 July the aircraft was prepared for its first catapult launch. This took place without a hitch and so the trials continued until 13 July by which time 12 take off and landings had been accomplished.

Towards the end of July the aircraft returned to Bedford to carry out preparatory trials for carrier operations with various stores fitted.

On 20 October the second series of trials began aboard the Clemenceau, and it was during these trials that disaster very nearly struck.

The aircraft failed to catch the arrestor wire and was struggling to gain enough power to lift cleanly from the deck in order to make another approach to the wire. The pilot just managed to keep the aircraft from hitting the water and managed to make a successful landing on the second attempt. The cause of the near crash was put down to the slow response from the throttle and engines which left the French Naval officials less than impressed.

Another problem that was creeping in was the growing development costs which would mean that only half the planned order would be able to be bought. Even more so when the final cost was measured against purchasing A-4 Skyhawks or A-7 Corsairs from the US. Finally the Navy's patience snapped and they announced that they would be buying the Super Etendard, against the wishes of the French Government. The Etendard was no better or worse than the Jaguar, but yet again it was the chance to buy a solely home grown product against one jointly developed with the British.

The prototype Jaguar M was then simply reduced to flying tests with the Navy before it made its last flight on 12 December 1975. It was delivered to Rochefort to become a ground instructional machine.

Making a slow pass over the deck of the Clemenceau is the prototype Jaguar M. This maritime variant differed by virtue of having single main wheels and twin nose wheels. The aircraft is finished in Navy Blue upper surfaces with White undersides. (BAe)

Maritime Jaguar M05 makes one of its catapult launches from the deck of the Clemenceau during the trials. The aircraft was not a success and the French Navy opted to buy the Super Etendard instead. Unusual for a carrier is the checkerboard covered caravan on the end of the deck. (BAe)

Export Jaguar

With a design as good as the Jaguar there was always going to be the possibility of export orders being placed by friendly nations who had a history of purchasing military equipment from both France and Great Britain. The 1974 SBAC show at Farnborough saw the official launch of the "Jaguar International" when the first aircraft for the RAF, an S1, serialed XX108, was displayed as the export version. The export aircraft would feature up rated engines, multi purpose Agave radar and a vast choice of offensive stores. By the time the aircraft had been displayed at the shows two orders were already forthcoming.

Oman

The air force of the Sultanate of Oman (Al Kuwait al Jawwiya al Sultanate Oman/SOAF) had a long tradition of operating British aircraft and so the choice of the Jaguar was a simple one. The order was announced on 28 August 1974 without naming the nation for 12 single seat strike and a pair two seat trainers. The first two aircraft being delivered in March 1977 with the delivery of all other aircraft completed by the end of July 1978.

The aircraft joined No. 8 Sqn at Masirah Island, just off the coast of mainland Oman. The aircraft were finished in a desert scheme of Stone and Dark Earth which was ideal for the terrain in which they would be operating. The low level nature of their role within the Omani Air Force was indicated by the fact that the aircraft carried much reduced size national insignia of a shield on the fin plus serials in both standard numbers and Arabic script.

In 1980 a follow on order was placed for a further 12 aircraft made up of 10 single seaters and two trainers. These aircraft were powered by the up rated Dash 58 engine which gave 40% better thrust in combat conditions without affecting the fuel consumption too much. The aircraft were delivered to No. 20 Sqn in 1983 with Low Vis national insignia painted on the fin, this time in Dark Blue.

The Omani aircraft were wired to carry the MATRA Magic 550 AAM's on over wing pylons but following a request by the air force these fittings were replaced with under wing rails allowing AIM-9P Sidewinders to be carried instead.

In 1990 the SOAF became known as the Royal Air Force of Oman (RAFO) as it moved forward with the changing times.

Following the 1990 invasion of Kuwait by Iraq the Omanis joined the Allied coalition against the Iraqi aggression but the ROAF Jaguars would play no active part in operations against Iraqi forces during Desert Storm.

Ecuador

Ordered at the same time as the Omani aircraft the Ecuadorian Government placed an order for 12 Jaguars, 10 single seat strike aircraft and two trainers. This followed initial interest that began in 1972. Prior to delivery six pilots from the Ecuadorian Air Force (Fuerza Aerea Ecuatoriana) underwent a conversion course with the RAF at Lossiemouth. This was part of the sales agreement that also included the RAF giving updated simulator training to FAE pilots every 18 months.

The first aircraft were delivered to Ecuador in January 1977, to Base Aerea Militar Tauranear Guayaquil in central Ecuador. There they equipped the FAE's only fighter wing, No. 21 Ala De Combate. The unit was known

as the "Eagles" whilst flying their previous mounts, the ageing Gloster Meteor F.8's, but soon changed their nickname to the "Jaguares" once the new aircraft arrived. The FAE aircraft were finished in the same camouflage as their French and British counterparts with the Light Grey undersides worn by the RAF aircraft in the early part of their careers. In a style often accepted by foreign air forces the national insignia was carried on the upper port wing only with large FAE letters on the opposite wing.

India

Without doubt the biggest export customer for the Jaguar was the Indian Air Force (Bharatiya Vayu Sena/IAF) who although wanted the aircraft in service quickly were delayed from buying the aircraft for some 12 years. The Indians had shown interest as far back as 1966 when the seeds were first sown but the actual signing of contracts did not occur until 1978.

This was due to the depth of study put into choosing the right aircraft for the IAF. The Jaguar came up against competition from the Mirage F.1 and SAAB Viggen before being chosen. The choice of the Jaguar came down to a number of factors. The Jaguar was the only twin engined aircraft offering better survivability, it was more economical and also the aircraft could be delivered on a schedule to suit the IAF. The factor that probably swung it most was the ability to build the Jaguar in India, a major political point in the bidding. The agreement was that India would buy direct the first 40 aircraft and build another 120 "in country". They would borrow 18 aircraft from the RAF to allow crews to do a local conversion course onto the aircraft. The Jaguar was to replace both the Hunter and Canberra in IAF service which may not be a major task for a Hunter pilot but would be a whole new ball game to a pilot used to flying the larger Canberra.

The Jaguar S1 "International" displayed in the static park at Farnborough in 1974. Displayed along with the weapon options is the optional nose fit offered initially to export customers. The badge just below the cockpit is a British Industry Award. The S1 was more akin to a French A model, having no RWR on the fin or Laser Rangefinder fitted in the nose. (BAe)

On 19 July 1979 the first two interim aircraft were handed over to the Indians at Warton with the remaining aircraft being delivered to India over the following six weeks. The aircraft joined No. 14 Sqn based at Ambala in the North of the country. When deliveries of aircraft purposely built for the IAF started in February 1981 they joined No. 14 Sqn, bringing "The Bulls" as they are known, up to full operational strength. The second unit to receive the Jaguar was No. 5 Sqn, "The Tuskers", also based at Ambala.

The IAF aircraft were finished in a similar camouflage scheme as the wrap round adopted by the RAF. Next to form was No. 27 Sqn, "The Flaming Arrows", who traded in their Hunters for the new aircraft early in 1985. These were the first locally built Jaguars to enter service. All of the IAF nicknames refer to the colorful badges worn on the aircraft which hark back to a similar style to those of RAF units during the 1950's, a much more colorful period in aviation history. The license built aircraft were manufactured by Hindustan Aircraft (HAL). Following on from No. 27 Sqn were No. 16, "The Cobras", who replaced their Canberras for the smaller more agile type while relocating to a new base at Gorakhpur in October 1986.

The IAF considered further additional squadrons but these were never introduced to operate the standard GR.1 type. The Aircraft & Systems Testing Establishment based at Bangalore operate a few single and twin seat aircraft for trials purposes.

The one aspect where the IAF stands out is in its use of the Jaguar as a maritime attack aircraft. To offer this type of mission No. 6 Sqn, "The Dragons", were formed at Poona in 1987. These aircraft were modified to carry the Agave radar enclosed in a conical nose cone. Eight aircraft were fitted with this new nose and radar, which has a range of 70 nautical miles against sea borne targets and 15 miles against airborne ones. Also the aircraft carry the Sea Eagle Anti-Ship Missile on the centerline pylon. Designated the Jaguar International IM the aircraft are instantly recognizable and also the fact that they are finished in a different camouflage makes them stand out from the rest of the IAF fleet. They wear a unique two tone Blue wrap around scheme.

India has been the biggest export operator of the Jaguar. Here one of the Warton built aircraft, J1003, departs from the airfield. This aircraft was one of several loaned to the Indians. (BAe)

Lined up at an airbase in India are a full compliment of Jaguars. All are finished in standard RAF colors and identical to the RAF's GR.1. (David James)

Nigeria

Probably the most surprising export order was that from the African state of Nigeria who had previously bought most of its military aircraft from the Soviet Union. In early 1983 the Nigerian Government placed an order for 18 aircraft made up of 13 single seat and five trainers. There was also an option held for ordering a further 18 in the future.

The first four aircraft were handed over in May 1984 and used for a brief conversion course held in the UK for the Nigerian pilots. Later that year the remaining aircraft started to be delivered to Makurdi Air Base in southern central Nigeria. The aircraft were operated by an un-named squadron, replacing MiG-17's, under the guidance of NAF Strike Command which later became Tactical Air Command.

For operations in this part of the world the aircraft were camouflaged in a three color wrap round scheme of Sand, Light Green and Dark Green. Due to the almost paranoid security of some of these nations and their defense forces very little can be gleaned about the day to day operations of the aircraft in NAF service. But the poor state of the economies has been shown by the failure to replace any of the four aircraft known to have been lost in accidents; also the option for the follow on order has never been taken up due to similar reasons. Had the follow on order been

The shimmering lake and snow capped mountains offer a stunning backdrop to this Indian AF Jaguar of No. 14 Sqn IAF. The unit is known as "The Bulls" carries a charging bull on the unit badge seen just aft of the intake. (BAe)

India is the only nation to operate the Jaguar in a maritime role. This Jaguar IM of No. 6 Sqn is seen at an air show in India. The Agave radar being mounted in a modified nose cone, one of only eight IM's built. (David James)

placed six of these aircraft would have been fitted with the Agave radar as carried by the Indian maritime aircraft.

Failed Export Bids

Despite interest and sales from various corners of the world the Jaguar has been shelved or dropped for various reasons by other potential operators.

In Europe, Belgium had considered buying into the Anglo-French SEPECAT deal but later changed its mind. Another NATO member, Turkey, considered buying the Jaguar to bring its air force into line with other more modern allies. They tried to raise the finance to buy the Jaguar via Libya in 1975 but the deal fell through and the Turks were left to soldier on with their ageing F-100 Super Sabres.

Whilst one Arab nation bought the Jaguar another did not, for different reasons. Kuwait was interested in the type but after publicly stating they would purchase 50 Jaguars and 16 Mirage F.1's they suddenly dropped their interest in the Jaguar. Another Gulf State, Abu Dhabi, were intending to buy Jaguars instead of adding more Mirages to its air force but following some dirty tactics, the deal collapsed and Abu Dhabi not surprisingly bought more Mirages! These types of tactics are not uncommon for the French when it comes to selling military equipment, especially if they were competing against British companies, showing the long standing economic fued between the nations.

A similar thing happened when the Pakistan Air Force indicated an interest in buying Jaguars, if the US would not supply A-7 Corsairs. They later placed an order for Mirages. An indication of just how committed the French side of SEPECAT were to export the aircraft, in competition to its Mirages, can be borne out of the fact that all of the export sales were generated by the British side of the consortium.

Omani ground crew service a GR.1 in one of the HASs that protect the Omani aircraft from any attacks. The aircraft are finished in a desert scheme, along with all the ground equipment too! The aircraft is armed with AIM-9 Sidewinders under the outer rails. (BAe)

No. 8 Sqn is the operator of these five aircraft, based at Masirah Island just off the bottom of Oman. The only markings carried are the Omani crest on the fin in red, and the serial number in both numerals and Arabic script. All stencils are in English. (BAe)

Hammering down the runway on a damp British day this Jaguar trainer is leaving for a much warmer and drier climate in the Gulf. This is one of the first two T.2's supplied to Oman, later ones were fitted with RWR on the fin. (BAe)

A line up of a later batch of Jaguars ready for handover to the ROAF. In the foreground is a two seater fitted with RWR, the Omani two seaters being unique in this. Also the color of the national insignia has changed to blue instead of red on the crest. These aircraft were delivered in 1983. (David James)

FAE302 makes a graceful descent over the River Guayas Delta as the "Jaguare" makes its way back to its lair. The Grey in the camouflage is starting to fade in this photo and the under wing tank also shows signs of serious chipping. Note the large FAE identification on the upper wing. (BAe)

Heading from Warton to South America, a pair of Jaguar GR.1's on delivery to the Ecuadorian Air Force. Ecuador is the only South American operator of this type. These immaculate aircraft are finished in the early RAF grey/green scheme with light grey undersides. (David James).

Possibly due to the different terrain color or the effects of sun on the Light Grey, but the FAE Jaguars have gradually changed their coats. FAE318 sports Olive Drab instead of Grey in a new overall wrap around scheme. Also the style of lettering has changed. (BAe)

(Below) FAE302 was the second aircraft delivered to Ecuador. It is based at Taura with Escuadron de Combate 2111. This Jaguar is on a training sortie west of Playas. (BAe)

The most unusual, and secretive, operator of the Jaguar is Nigeria. This single seater is on a test flight prior to delivery, indicated by the stenciled number on the fuselage, thought to be 827-392. Very little is known about the operations within the Nigerian Air Force, but some losses have occurred. (BAe)

(Below) Basking in the low winter sun is T.2 NAF700 prior to delivery to the Nigerian Air Force at Makurdi. The NAF aircraft are finished in a scheme of Sand, Medium Green and Dark Green, not unlike the USAF SE Asia scheme in terms of pattern. (BAe)

The Nigerian Air Force had usually purchased its military equipment from the Soviet Union, making the purchase of the Jaguar quite an unusual step for this African nation. NAF700, is the first two seater to be delivered to the NAF. (BAe)

ACT Jaguar

As part of the ongoing development of the aircraft control systems BAe modified a single GR.1, XX765, to Fly-By-Wire configuration using an all digital quadruplex system, the first aircraft to have this system. The system meant that no mechanical reversion system was fitted and the aircraft would basically be unstable without the constant adjustments made by the controls following commands from the central computer.

To make the aircraft unstable four tons of ballast were added to the rear portion of the fuselage to make the FBW system work constantly. The aim was to develop more maneuverable aircraft for future combat use, such as the Typhoon Euro fighter.

Resplendent in its Red, White and Blue color scheme, XX765 flew for the first time in the new configuration on 20 October 1981 from Warton. The aircraft performed very well on this initial flight considering the modifications made to it, and much new information was gleaned from this flight.

By the time of the fifth series of tests, in March of 1984, the aircraft had been fitted with large leading badge strakes, added to further destabilize the aircraft, and the Fly-By-Wire (FBW) markings on the fin had given way to new Active-Control-Technology (ACT) markings.

Further tests were carried out that year before the aircraft was retired and placed into storage. A good many factors and lessons were learned that have been incorporated into the systems design of the Typhoon which is now entering service with the RAF.

Two years later and the same aircraft now wears the new title of ACT on the fin. The leading edge extensions on the wing can be seen as the aircraft prepares to display at Farnborough. (Author)

GR.1, XX765, was used for the Fly-By-Wire trials on the type. Seen here in 1982 the aircraft wore a Red, White, Blue scheme with FBW title on the fin. The aircraft is on a test flight from Warton, passing over Blackpool, where the Tower can be seen behind the aircraft. (BAe)

Lifting off on another test flight is the ACT Jaguar and from this angle the wing leading edge extensions can clearly be seen. (BAe)

Combat

1991 Desert Shield

Following the Iraqi invasion of Kuwait on 2 August 1990 the United Nations deployed forces to various bases around the Persian Gulf in order to try and halt any further aggression by Saddam Hussein's regime. Amongst the first deployed to the region were 12 Jaguar GR.1As from Coltishall on 11 August under OPERATION GRANBY flying to Thumrait in Oman to form the Jaguar Wing. The aircraft were rotated between the Gulf and the UK along with crews in November with the intention being that crews served six month tours of duty in the Gulf region.

Shortly after the RAF deployment the first French aircraft began to arrive as eight Jaguar As from EC 11 deployed on 15 and 17 October to Al Ahsa in Eastern Saudi Arabia. Unlike their British comrades some of the French pilots already had combat experience in desert conflicts, having flown missions in Chad. The French build up was brought together under OPERATION DAGUET.

For various reasons the Omani Jaguars were not included in the build up to the Gulf War.

Almost immediately after arriving in the region the pilots began flying familiarization sorties over the new terrain and adapting to the much higher temperatures in the Gulf. The RAF aircraft incorporated a number of modifications to the aircraft based in the UK. Most obvious was the fitting of the overwing rails to allow a pair of AIM-9L Sidewinders to be carried for self defense, a feature only seen on export aircraft before. For passive self defense the aircraft were fitted with the ALQ-101 jamming pod and Phimat chaff dispensers. The French aircraft carried a single Matra Magic 550 missile as well as Phimat chaff dispensers and ESD Barax ECM pods.

Once combat missions began the Jaguars would be tasked with raids against important targets, mainly in Kuwait, including Iraqi armored units, missile sites and naval vessels. For these missions they would carry a selection of ordnance including 1,000lb bombs, AS 30L ASM, Belouga and Rockeye Cluster Bombs.

Desert Storm

With the start of the air campaign against Iraqi forces on 15 January 1991 Jaguars of both the RAF and Armee de l'Air were thrown straight into the action. The opening day saw four RAF GR.1As attack Iraqi Army barracks in Kuwait using two 1,000lb bombs dropped from each aircraft. This smaller load was due to the fact that all aircraft carried underwing fuel tanks, which were soon exchanged for a single centerline tank, allowing more ordnance to be carried. The same morning saw 12 French aircraft attack the Scud Missile depot at Ahmed Al Jaber AB in Kuwait. The French dropping Belouga cluster bombs and 250Kg bombs. During this raid one aircraft sustained damage from an SA-7 Anti Aircraft Missile. The strike causing a major fire around the lower rear fuselage whilst another aircraft was hit by an AAA round, causing slight damage. Both aircraft diverted to Jubail in Northern Saudi Arabia. Another aircraft had been hit in the canopy by small arms fire. The pilot, possibly the luckiest jaguar pilot around, found that the round had actually gone through part of his helmet without injuring him seriously.

As the intensive air strikes continued to soften up the Iraqi forces in both Kuwait and their homeland the Jaguars from both air forces continued to carry out missions against enemy

Combat in the 1991 Gulf War showed that the Jaguar was a very capable combat aircraft. Prior to deployment, the aircraft were given a Desert Pink scheme which already looks somewhat tatty. This aircraft, XZ113/FD, is from No. 41 Sqn. The fitting of overwing AIM-9 rails was an unusual move for the RAF aircraft. (BAe)

The same aircraft on the same training flight. All of the RAF's Jaguar detachment to the Gulf came under the command of the Coltishall Wing, which drew aircraft and crews from the various RAF Jaguar squadrons. (BAe)

installations without suffering any further damage to the aircraft. On 22 January French aircraft attacked three Iraqi ships berthed in the Kuwaiti Naval base using AS 30L missiles causing substantial damage.

Following the start of Iraqi use of Scud Missiles to launch attacks against Saudi Arabia and Israel the allies began the great Scud Hunt. RAF Jaguars were given a secondary tasking of assisting in this and for these missions they were fitted with a centerline recce pod.

On 26 January RAF Jaguars, along with Tornados, undertook a series of raids against the various Iraqi Silkworm Missile batteries based in Kuwait. This was part of the plan to fool the Iraqis into thinking that the Allies intended to liberate Kuwait via a sea borne invasion.

30 January saw RAF Jaguars carry out a varied range of missions against enemy landing craft operating just off the Kuwaiti coastline. Using the CRV7 High Velocity Rockets carried in pods under the wings three craft were sunk. Later the same day eight aircraft attacked an Iraqi gun battery north of Kuwait City whilst another five struck at one of the main command posts in the area. By this time the French Jaguars were striking deeper into Iraq following the approval of the French government. They were joined on these missions by Mirage F1's that had previously been restricted in their operations due to the possibility of them being confused with enemy aircraft.

The following day another landing craft fell victim to RAF Jaguars working in unison with US Navy A-6's. It had previously been hit by a Sea Skua missile fired from HMS Gloucester. Indeed the Jaguar was certainly proving its value as a potent strike aircraft despite its age and the doubts expressed in certain circles before the war.

On 3 February a number of RAF Jaguars attacked the small Iraqi garrison on the island of Faylakah before Kuwaiti troops landed to retake it. Although of little military importance it was the first piece of Kuwaiti soil to be liberated from the enemy. Now the aircraft of both nations turned to one of the most important stages of the war, the preparation for the land offensive.

Filling up on the way out to the Gulf. Vital support to the RAF's strike aircraft came from its fleet of Victor and VC10 tanker aircraft. A Jaguar refuels from a VC10 while another waits its turn. (Paul Jackson)

Heading out to war, with Mount Etna in the background. RAF Jaguar pilots had to make long flights out to the Gulf region. The overwing rails can be seen without the AIM-9's and the only under wing stores are fuel tanks. (Paul Jackson)

The RAF Jaguar fleet operated well with the Tornado's from the UK. Three GR.1's accompany a Tornado GR.1 to refuel from a VC10K.2 tanker over the Gulf during Desert Storm. (Author)

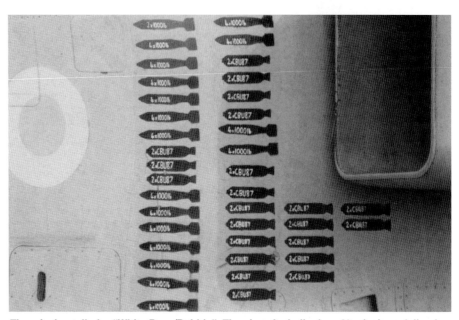

XZ367/GP saw action throughout the conflict. Originally from No. 54 Sqn the aircraft was given the artwork and name "White Rose". It was originally "Debbie", one of a number painted by Cpl Paul Robbins. A camouflaged tank is carried under the wing, RAF Mildenhall in 1991. (Author)

Because of the possible threat to Allied aircraft from Iraqi interceptors the aircraft were fitted with overwing Sidewinder rails. This allowed the aircraft to also carry ECM pods on the outer pylons, while retaining the self defense capability of the AIM-9. (Author)

The mission tally for "White Rose/Debbie". The aircraft chalked up 40 missions delivering death and destruction to enemy forces. The aircraft used various types of bombs and in different quantities as can be seen from the details included on the mission tally. (Author)

The mission tally for GR.1 XZ106 which flew a mix of ground attack sorties and recce missions. The three camera symbols indicate the recce missions whilst the others show the use of bombs and on one occasion the use of rockets against enemy positions. Most intriguing is the AIM-9 Sidewinder kill...used against a truck! (Paul Jackson)

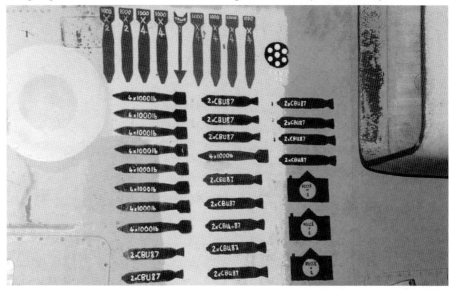

Desert Storm saw the RAF show a new degree of tolerance for various types of artwork on its combat aircraft. Many crews opted for scantily clad females such as "Katrina Jane" painted on the nose of XZ119. (Paul Jackson)

Apart from the sexually suggestive artwork some showed the British sense of humor to its cheekiest levels. Here XX962/X was adorned with the "FAT SLAGS" two not-so sexually impressive ladies featured in the British adult comic Viz at the time. (Paul Jackson)

"MARY ROSE", XZ356/N, flew 33 missions during the war and showed somewhat restrained artwork compared to many other RAF Jaguars. (Paul Jackson)

Another character from Viz was featured on Jaguar XZ118/Y. BUSTER GONAD flew against the Iraqis on 38 occasions. The image and text beneath the wheelbarrow says it all! Typical British postcard humor at its best. (Paul Jackson)

43

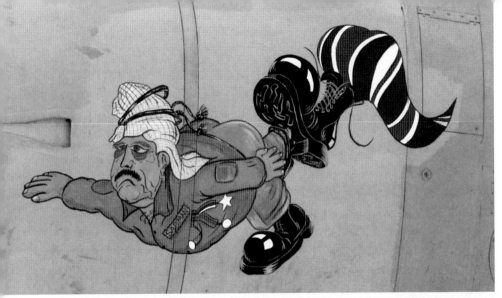

One of most politically motivated was this cartoon of "Sadman" being given the order of the boot by the British. Indeed from this close up the level of detail incorporated into some of the artwork was very impressive, but we are not sure just what the Bagdahd authorities of the day thought of it. This artwork adorned GR.1A XZ364/Q which carried out 40 missions during Desert Storm. (Paul Jackson)

Viewed as the biggest threat to an Allied success was the Iraqi Republican Guard who had a reputation of being great fighters, but it turned out to be a lot of bark, with little bite. The Republican Guard was dug in along the Kuwait/Saudi border and became the victims of possibly the most intensive bombing campaign since the Second World War. They were bombed day and night with the intention being to totally demoralize them, leaving them wide open to a fast and bloody advance by Allied forces. In the build up to the ground offensive Jaguars carried out daily raids against Iraqi ground forces and their support services as part of the massive Allied air offensive.

Amongst the targets identified and attacked were various communication centers that linked the enemy front line, troop concentrations and bridges by which the enemy could supply and support frontline troops. As soon as the Iraqis replaced a damaged bridge the Jaguars would take it out again.

Throughout February the aircraft flew missions carrying recce pods, but with one modification. The line scanner was replaced by an F126 camera. This gave low-level photo reconnaissance information. A second aircraft would carry a Vinten VICON optical pod and this pair of aircraft would often fly as pathfinders for conventionally armed aircraft allowing the attack to take place, but also gathering information about the raid and subsequent damage caused.

Once the ground offensive got underway British and French Jaguars started to rove much further north in search of chaos to cause, and this often meant inflicting severe damage to Saddam's supply routes for this troops.

By the time a ceasefire was in place the RAF Jaguar fleet had flown 618 sorties without a single loss, dropping 750 bombs, 393 cluster bombs, firing 608 rockets and 9,600 rounds of ammunition. The French aircraft flew 615 sorties with two aircraft damaged. They dropped a similar amount of ordnance as the RAF aircraft had. And on completion of Desert Storm the aircraft of both nations left for home in March of that year.

44

A job well done, RAF Jaguars returned to Coltishall shortly after the end of hostilities in the Gulf. The pilot of XZ358/W "Diplomatic Service" has his canopy open and is ready to await the crew ladder so he can have a very much deserved home coming. Note the Grey colored Recce pod on the centerline pylon. (Paul Jackson).

A close up of the nose area shows the extent of the weathering as well as the artwork and mission tally. The aircraft flew a fairly balanced mix of ground attack and recce sorties during Desert Storm, amassing a total of 14 missions. (Paul Jackson)

Back home from the war, and parked up at the dispersal at Coltishall is GR.1A XZ364/Q "Sadman". Although the general appearance of the desert scheme does not seem too bad the paint was very susceptible to the conditions and faded badly as well as chipping away from areas such as leading edges and the wing tanks. (Paul Jackson)

Taxiing in to an emotional home coming from families and friends was the last piece in the jigsaw for Gulf war Jaguar pilots. XZ118/Y is guided into a slot at the dispersal at Cotishall. The heavy weathering and exhaust staining much in evidence on the rear fuselage. The hangar behind belongs to No. 41 Sqn, but the Coltishall Wing was the overall command under which the "Desert Cats" flew. (Paul Jackson)

Post War. Back to business. A pair of Jaguars from No. 6 Sqn on a training sortie. The desert finished aircraft carrying standard camouflaged tanks while the other aircraft, in full squadron colors, has desert tanks. Both aircraft carry 1,000lb bombs under the centerline pylons. On the desert camouflaged aircraft the "Flying Canopeners" badge can barely be seen on the forward nose in red. (Paul Jackson)

As ground crew secure the aircraft its pilot has a very emotional reunion with a loved one. The worn appearance of the wing tanks can be seen and also the black nose wheel door. On the undersides a fake canopy had been painted to confuse Iraqi anti aircraft gunners. (Paul Jackson)

Operation Warden

With the end of Desert Storm the Allies started to withdraw from the region hopeful that the downfall of Saddam Hussein would come from within Iraqis borders. This failed to happen and thinking that the UN would not interfere with internal conflicts Iraqi units began a series of attacks against the Kurds in the north and the Shi-ites in the south of the country. In the past the Iraqis had thought nothing of using chemical weapons to quell any uprisings from these parts of its country. As the attacks grew in ferocity it became clear that the UN would have to take action in order to get humanitarian aid to the people of these regions.

In the north "Operation Warden" got under way with the UN declaring a No Fly zone indicating that any Iraqi intrusions into the zone would be dealt with, which basically says, "If You Fly – You Die". The main base for these operations was the US base at Incirlik in Turkey and to assist the operation eight RAF Jaguar GR.1As were deployed. The aircraft were in place by early September 1991 and began flying reconnaissance missions over Iraq operating with French and US aircraft.

XX766/EA of No. 6 Sqn shows the extent of weathering sustained by the desert scheme which was a temporary paint job applied over the standard camouflage. The way the panel lines are accentuated is very similar to that on US Navy/USMC aircraft. The aircraft is seen over the North Sea on a training mission. After the end of hostilities Jaguars continued to operate from Incirlik on missions over the No Fly Zones in Iraq. (Paul Jackson)

When undertaking recce patrols over the No-Fly zones in Iraq the Jaguars were fitted with the standard recce camera pod under the centerline pylon. A member of the air photographic section changes the rolls of film carried on the missions. (Paul Jackson)

Post sortie analysis is undertaken by photo specialists trained to look for infringements by the Iraqis. The raised viewer gives the Sergeant a perspective similar to looking at a 3-D image. (Paul Jackson)

French participation in Desert Storm, or Operation Daguet, was on a smaller scale to that of the British Jaguar force. This very weathered A from EC4/11 is seen on a sortie over the Gulf. Initially the FAF Jaguars only attacked targets in Kuwait on orders from Paris. (Thomson-CSF). (Author).

A very weathered example, A95, from EC2/11 sits at its home base at Bordeaux France. French paint faded very quickly in the Gulf giving a much more subtle camouflage scheme to the aircraft. The undersides are very also heavily weathered. (Author)

A1/7-IA from EC3/7 was part of the French Jaguar force in the Gulf, seen on their return to France. The scheme being faded somewhat and the small shark badge on the fin almost impossible to make out. French Jaguars flew 615 sorties during the war suffering no combat losses. (David James)

For these recce missions the aircraft would carry the Vinten VICON pod. Air to air refueling support came from RAF VC10K.2 and Victor K.2 tankers. The missions were really a show of strength and deterrent while other units were flying mercy missions dropping food and clothing to the displaced population.

The RAF Jaguar commitment to this role carried on for two years until the aircraft were replaced by Harriers in April 1993.

OPERATION TELIC

When the US and British led invasion of Iraq happened in 2003 there was a small RAF Jaguar GR.3 detachment deployed to Incirlik in Turkey. The aircraft, from No. 6 Sqn at Coltishall, were all given an overall camouflage scheme of Light Grey ARTF (Alkaline Removable Temporary Finish) with toned down insignia. Having been deployed to Turkey they then found that the Turkish Government would not allow operations to be flown from the base during the war. So it is unknown if any aircraft played any part in the Iraqi campaign of 2003.

Senegal and Chad

Along with the British, the French have always maintained strong links with some of their former colonies around the world, particularly those in Africa. Whilst not directly involving themselves in the day to day running of these countries they have always offered support, often in a military sense.

The former French colony of Senegal became an Armee de l'Air Jaguar base for a short time in late 1977 to early 1978 as aircraft thought to be from EC.11 were flying missions under OPERATION LAMANTIN to carry out strikes against positions held by Polisario Front guerrillas who were launching raids against Mauritanian territory in the former Spanish Sahara.

The guerrillas were armed with various weapons, probably supplied by the Soviet Union and Libya, and during the first month of action two Jaguars were shot down by ground fire from the guerrillas. A third aircraft was lost the following May during a raid against Polisario positions. With the growing unrest the Mauritanian Government relinquished its claim, bringing peace, of a sort, to the region.

When operating in the deserts of Africa or the Gulf, the Jaguars blend in well with their surroundings. Jaguar A of EC3/11 takes off from a desert strip. The unit has seen combat in Senegal and Lebanon as well as Desert Storm. (Sirpa Air)

(Above Left) In other regions such as North Africa the French have used Jaguars on a number of occasions to defend French interests. This desert camouflaged A from EC4/11 comes into land. This unit has seen action in Chad and Senegal against Libyan backed guerrillas. (David James)

When NATO went to war against Yugoslavia over Kosovo RAF Jaguars were again used in combat. They adopted the lo-vis scheme of two shades of Grey. This GR.3 is seen on a training sortie, over terrain not unlike that of the Balkans. (David James)

Throughout much of the Balkan conflict the RAF Jaguar force took part in patrols or combat missions against Serb forces, firstly over Bosnia then against Serbia during the Kosovo Conflict. Seen here is an RAF GR.3 over the sea. As part of the extended self protection against ground fire or SAM's flare dispensers are fitted under the fuselage. This Jaguar is on a training sortie carrying practice bomb carriers under the outer pylons. (BAe)

The Jaguar GR.3 took part in joint operations with RAF Harrier GR.5's over Yugoslavia. The Jaguars provided the laser range finding and designation for the Harriers, operating as "Pathfinders". Based in Italy the aircraft only had a short flight across the Adriatic to targets in the former Yugoslavia. (RAF)

As the action in one region of Africa came to an end so another started when in early 1978 Libyan backed Froliant guerrillas launched a series of attacks against Chad Government forces in defiance of previously agreed, and signed, ceasefire documents.

Aircraft and support crews from EC.11 were then deployed to N'djamena in Chad under the mission of OPERATION TACUD. From the base there they carried out a number of missions against guerrilla units operating from bases inside Libya. On 31 May an aircraft was shot down by an SA-7 "Grail" SAM whilst carrying out a raid. During that same year another three aircraft were lost. By the early part of 1980 the guerrilla force was in control of much of the country and had almost taken over completely, indeed to the level of forming its own government. With the things going against them the French withdrew some of their forces from the country, but still maintained a presence in Chad. The force was retained there as a rapid reaction force that could respond to any request for assistance from friendly countries in the region.

In 1983 war flared up again in Chad and as part of the French declaration of a "Red Line" to separate the warring factions French Jaguars once more began to fly patrols over the region. The deployment went without incident as far as the Jaguar force was concerned until January 1984 when an aircraft was shot down by 23mm cannon fire whilst attacking a rebel convoy. A further aircraft was lost in a non combat accident in May, shortly before the French units withdrew.

1986 saw French Jaguars return once more to the region as the Libyans had assisted the rebels in building an airbase in the Northern part of Chad at adi Doum. This breach of frontiers by the Libyans sent alarm bells ringing in the Chad capital, and a request was made to Paris for help. In response the French began launching raids from Bangui against the base using Jaguars and other types, starting on 16 February. Using the BAP-100 Cluster Bombs they seriously damaged the Wadi Doum runway, mainly in an attempt to stop Libyan AF aircraft from operating there in support of rebel forces. Under OPERATION EPERVIER the French continued to fly surveillance missions over the area with the loss of one aircraft. A further raid was mounted in January 1987 when Martel missiles were used to destroy Libyan radar installations at the base. This was the last action as a ceasefire was signed shortly afterwards, which has held to date.

El Alto Cenepa

A border dispute between Ecuador and Peru had been the cause of a number of small clashes between the two nations between 1941 and 1981. On 26 January 1995 war broke out between the two nations once again when Ecuadorian troops crossed the border to claim the territory. The air forces of both sides began operations in support of their armies.

It's not recorded what, if any, action the FAE Jaguars were involved in, but it seems certain that the aircraft would have undertaken sorties, operating alongside Mirage F.1's and Kfirs against Peruvian forces. Lasting about a month this brief conflict saw the FAE getting the better of the FAP in terms of combat losses with only one A-37 damaged, compared to seven known losses for the FAP.

Balkans

At the start of the 1990's the former state of Yugoslavia began to break up as the various member states all demanded independence from Belgrade. Nations such as Slovenia and Croatia fought short but bloody wars to gain their freedom but one region that stood out amongst the others for the violence and brutality was Bosnia-Herzegovina. One of the biggest areas it was split between Muslims, Croats and Serbs and much of the tension was gathered around the capital Sarajevo.

With the growing bloodshed and atrocities the United Nations deployed forces to the region in a vain attempt to keep the peace, or to try and bring peace! As part of the air power deployed the RAF sent 12 Jaguars GR.1As from RAF Coltishall. The aircraft departed on the afternoon of 16 July 1993 and headed for the Italian base of Gioia Del Colle where they would operate alongside RAF and Italian Tornados.

Under "Operation Deny Flight" the Jaguars were given a new tactical camouflage scheme of overall Light Grey with low Vis Pink/Light Blue national insignia. The aircraft were fitted with Phimat and ALQ-101 pods and over wing rails, although missiles were not carried. As well as the British Jaguars the French deployed eight aircraft from EC3/11 to Istrana Air Base in Italy as part of their contingent.

Later a pair of GR.1Bs from No: 54 Sqn were deployed to Gioia Del Colle with the other British aircraft there.

In 1994 NATO began OPERATION BLUE SWORD when military operations against Bosnian Serb forces were carried out. During Blue Sword RAF Jaguars saw action in a couple of missions against Serb Armor around Sarajevo and on a raid against Udbina Airbase in Serb Karajina. On both missions the aircraft used 1,000lb iron bombs.

As the situation got even more volatile in the region the Allies began "Operation Deliberate Force" in 1995 with even more missions against the Belgrade backed Serb forces in Bosnia. NO. 54 Sqn Jaguars were being operated in conjunction with the RAF Harrier GR.7's on missions against Serb targets. The Jaguars would designate and "light up" the target for the Paveway carrying Harriers to launch their attacks against; this was due to the Harrier not having its own laser designator. During one of these path finding missions a Jaguar was lost on 21 June 1995 over the Adriatic. The pilot ejected and was rescued with the cause being attributed to engine failure, and not combat.

During the Gulf war the Jaguars did not see combat but were on stand-by at Incirlik, Turkey.

Although the aircraft were not used operationally during the Second Gulf War, they were on standby at Incirlik in Turkey. This GR.3 with a recce pod is on standby in an HAS. (via Andy Evans)

As this GR.3 banks away the full underside of the aircraft can be seen. The aircraft has an empty centerline pylon which usually carried either a recce pod or bombs. (via Andy Evans)

Prior to the Balkan war the RAF Jaguar fleet was given a new camouflage scheme of overall Gray with toned national insignia. (via Andy Evans)

More In Action

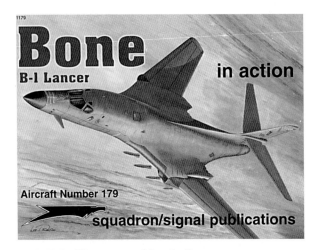

1179 Bone B-1 Lancer

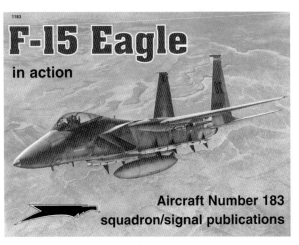

1183 F-15 Eagle

1178 B-2 Spirit

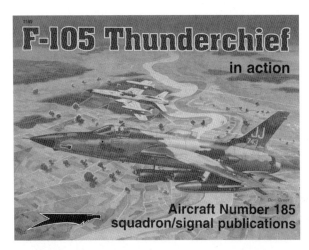

1185 F-105 Thunderchief

1168 AH-1 COBRA

1196 F-16 Fighting Falcon